GOD FIRST

GENESEE ABBEY LIBRARY
Piffard, New York

Bert Ghezzi and Peter Williamson
General Editors

God First

*What It Means to
Love God above All Things*

Ken Wilson

BV 4639 W52 1980 glas
Wilson, Ken.
God first : what it means to love

Computer ID: 51150

Servant Books
Ann Arbor, Michigan

Copyright © 1980 by Ken Wilson
All rights reserved.

Published by Servant Books
         P.O. Box 8617
         Ann Arbor, Michigan 48107

Cover Photo: Editorial Photocolor Archives
Book Design: John B. Leidy

Scripture quotations are taken from the *Revised Standard Version*, copyright 1946, 1953, © 1971, 1973 by the Division of Christian Education of the National Council of the Churches of Christ in the U.S.A.; the *New International Version* copyright © 1978 by New York International Bible Society, all rights reserved; the *New American Standard Bible* copyright © 1960, 1962, 1963, 1968, 1971, 1972, 1973, The Lockman Foundation, all rights reserved; *The New English Bible* © 1961, 1970, the Delegates of the Oxford University Press and the Syndics of the Cambridge University Press.

Where portions of the scripture quotations appear in italics, the emphasis has been added by the author.

Printed in the United States of America

ISBN 0-89283-089-1

Contents

Living as a Christian

In human terms, it is not easy to decide to follow Jesus Christ and to live our lives as Christians. Jesus requires that we surrender our selves to him, relinquish our aspirations for our lives, and submit our will to God. Men and women have never been able to do this easily; if we could, we wouldn't need a savior.

Once we accept the invitation and decide to follow Jesus, a new set of obstacles and problems assert themselves. We find that we are often ignorant about what God wants of us as his sons and daughters. For example, what does it mean practically to obey the first commandment — to love God with our whole mind, heart, and strength? How can we know God's will? How do we love people we don't like? How does being a Christian affect what we do with our time and money? What does it mean "to turn the other cheek?" In these areas — and many others — it is not easy to understand exactly what God wants.

Even when we do know what God wants, it can be quite difficult to apply his teaching to our daily lives. Questions abound. How do we find time to pray regularly? How do we repair a relationship with someone we have wronged or who has wronged us? How do we handle unruly emotional reactions?

These are examples of perplexing questions about the application of Christian teaching to our daily lives.

Furthermore, we soon discover that Christians have enemies — the devil outside and the flesh within. Satan tempts us to sin; our inner urges welcome the temptation, and we find our will to resist steadily eroding.

Finally, we must overcome the world. We are trying to live in an environment that is hostile toward what Christians believe and how they live and friendly toward those who believe and do the opposite. The world in which we live works on our Christian resolve in many subtle ways. How much easier it is to think and act like those around us! How do we persevere?

There is a two-fold answer to these questions: To live successfully as Christians, we need both grace and wisdom. Both are freely available from the Lord to those who seek him.

As Christians we live by grace. The very life of God works in us as we try to understand God's teaching, apply it to our lives, and overcome the forces that would turn us aside from our chosen path. We always need grace, and grace is always there. The Lord is with us always, and the supply of his grace is inexhaustible.

Yet grace works with wisdom. Christians must *learn* a great deal about how to live according to God's will. We must study God's word in scripture, listen to Christian teaching, and reflect on our own experience and the experience of others. Many Christians today lack this kind of wisdom. This is the need which the *Living as a Christian* series is designed to meet.

The book you are reading is part of a series of books intended to help Christians apply the teaching of scripture to their lives. The authors of *Living as a Christian* books are pastoral leaders who have given this teaching in programs of Christian formation in various Christian communities. The teaching has stood the test of time. It has already helped many people grow as faithful servants of the Lord. We decided it was time to make this teaching available in book form.

All the *Living as a Christian* books seek to meet the following criteria:

- **Biblical.** The teaching is rooted in scripture. The authors and editors maintain that scripture is the word of God, and that it ought to determine what Christians believe and how they live.

- **Practical.** The purpose of the series is to offer down-to-earth advice about living as a Christian.

- **Relevant.** The teaching is aimed at the needs we encounter in our daily lives — at home, in school, on the job, in our day-to-day relationships.

- **Brief and Readable.** We have designed the series for busy people from a wide variety of backgrounds. Each of the authors presents profound Christian truths as simply and clearly as possible, and illustrates those truths by examples drawn from personal experience.

- **Integrated.** The books in the series comprise a unified curriculum on Christian living. They do not present differing views, but rather they take a consistent approach.

The format of the series makes it suitable for both individual and group use. The books in *Living as a Christian* can be used in such group settings as Sunday school classes, adult education programs, prayer groups, classes for teen-agers, women's groups, and as a supplement to Bible study.

The *Living as a Christian* series is divided into several sets of books, each devoted to a different aspect of Christian living. These sets include books on Christian maturity, emotions in the Christian life, the fruit of the Holy Spirit, Christian personal relationships, Christian service, and very likely, on other topics as well.

This book, *God First*, is part of a set of books which communicates essential Christian wisdom for maturing in Christ. To grow in living the Christian life, we must learn about faith, love of God, love of neighbor, and our identity as sons and daughters of God, to name just a few topics. To reach spiritual maturity, Christians must know how God enables us to overcome the obstacles that inevitably arise: our own wrongdoing, the power of the world, the flesh, and the devil. *God First* and other books in this set present practical, scripturally based teaching that will help you attain basic maturity in your Christian life.

The editors dedicate the *Living as a Christian* series to Christian men and women everywhere who have counted the cost and decided to follow Jesus Christ as his disciples.

Bert Ghezzi and Peter Williamson
General Editors

PREFACE

You already know that you are supposed to love God. But because love can seem so vague and God so vast, you may not always be sure just what it means to love him. Besides, the results so far have probably been mixed. There are special times when you feel great love for God—it seems the most natural thing in the world; but the very fact that these are special occasions belies a nagging inconstancy. In fact, every now and then, loving God may seem impossible. Whether you throw up your hands and say it aloud, or simply think it, the question inevitably comes up: "How can I ever love God?" A very good question and a good place to begin.

If you want to love God, you must be more than merely interested in loving him. Loving God must be your ideal of life. It must be your objective, your aim, the direction toward which everything in your life points. If loving God is not your ideal, then no amount of wisdom, insight, or spiritual power will enable you to love him. Making love for God your principal aim is the critical first step. Yet, surprisingly, it is a step that few Christians have consciously taken.

Whether or not they know it, everyone has an ideal of life. By nature, we are purposeful crea-tures. We inevitably set goals for ourselves and direct our resources toward achieving them. We pursue material goods and comforts, the good opinion of others, skills and knowledge, power and accomplishment, freedom from pain. Some ideal of life joins these goals together and makes them part of something larger than themselves. For example, if your goals are to own two nice cars, have a happy family, a comfortable home, well-educated children, a spotless reputation, nice friends, and influence in the community, then your ideal of life is probably "to be a success." It is all the more satisfying to achieve particular goals when they fit into the overall ideal.

Perhaps you have never thought about what your ideal of life is, let alone what it ought to be. Nevertheless, everyone operates with some ideal for their life. Perhaps you picked up yours from your parents or close friends. You may have conflicting ideals which result in conflicting goals and considerable frustration. Perhaps your ideal is still "to be a success" only now this ideal has been translated into Christian terms: being respected by other Christians, knowing scripture well, having a regular prayer time, and so on. Whatever your ideal of life has been, it falls far short of the mark if it has not been to love the Lord with all your heart, mind, and strength.

Since the time of Moses, this has been the explicit ideal of God's people. In Jesus' day, pious Jews articulated this by praying a special prayer called the Shema each morning and evening. The core of the Shema, Hebrew for "hear," is from Deuteronomy, "Hear, O Israel: The Lord our God is one Lord; and you shall love the Lord your God with all your heart, and with all your soul, and with all your might" (6:4-5). The rabbis referred to this as the "yoke of the kingdom of heaven." When a Jew prayed the Shema, he was taking on this yoke. He was making the love of God his ideal of life.

Jesus quoted from the Shema when he was asked by a lawyer, "Which is the greatest commandment?" His answer—"You shall love the Lord your God with all your heart, and with all your soul, and with all your mind" (Mt 22:37)—is the Christian's ideal, his one aim in life.

Every other ideal fails to qualify, even such admirable ideals as "being a successful Christian," or "being a loving person," or "living up to my fullest potential." Loving God only works if we make it our one aim. Our God is jealous; he insists on being loved first and foremost.

If you want to love God, you must make this ideal, and no other, your guiding vision. You will need wisdom about what it means to love God and power to live by the ideal. But first, be certain about the ideal itself, and the reasons why it is the only thing worth spending your life on.

ONE

Why This Ideal?

Have you ever taken an important step or made an important decision because you had a notion that it was the right thing to do? That's not how you should approach deciding on your ideal of life. If you *think* that loving God is your aim in life, but you're not sure why it is, it's time to consider the reasons. If your ideal is something other than loving God, you should consider why it ought to change. If other ideals are competing with your desire to love God, now is the time to understand why loving God ought to be your ruling ideal. The reasons are simple, but knowing them will help you to make the ideal of loving God your explicit, clearly understood, and only aim in life.

God Is Worth It

"The kingdom of heaven is like a merchant in search of fine pearls, who, on finding one pearl of great value, went and sold all that he had and bought it" (Mt 13:45-46). We can imagine a seasoned pearl merchant traveling from town to town in search of the best buys. He enters a small shop on the seacoast where he finds a pearl unlike any he has ever seen. The price is enormous—as much as the combined value of his current stock—but the merchant knows a good pearl when he sees one. He is amazed that the pearl can be bought for any price, because he recognizes that this pearl is priceless.

In the kingdom of heaven's place of power sits one whose intrinsic value has captured the love and loyalty of men and women for thousands of years. He is the "ancient of days," the one who existed before the earth was created, who scattered the stars in the heavens and created the world and all it contains. To him, the scorching sun is like a plaything. He is the source of all that is truly good. Majesty, justice, and mercy surround his throne. He is the one who said to Abraham, "I am your shield and your very great reward." The author of life, he is also the savior of men. There is no greater understatement than to say, "nothing compares with him."

There are any number of ideals we might choose, or persons or things we might love above all else. It comes down to a question of who and what is worth it. We don't make loving God our aim because it seems like a decent alternative. We make loving God our aim because God deserves our love. His own worth and great love for us calls forth our response.

If you had $500 to spend on a wedding ring for your fiancee, and you had a choice between three rings—a sterling silver band, a gold-filled band with a small chip of jade, or a tastefully magnificent diamond—your choice would be easy. And if you had the opportunity to spend your life loving the all-powerful, all-knowing, all-good God or to spend it in pursuit of some other aim, what ideal could prove anything but a distant second best?

We Were Created to Love Him

Last year I bought a puppy for my family. He was a pleasant, playful Labrador—a dog with enough energy to keep up with my two oldest children, and custom-made, I thought, for us. Though I knew that the dog might well be a big one, I thought that daily runs with the children at a nearby park would provide a sufficient supplement to our backyard, which was admittedly small.

We named him "Lad", rather than "Tank", as a friend, who saw his potential for growth, suggested. Lad had a nice ring to it, but as it turned out, Tank would have been more descriptive. After a few months of Lad's phenomenal growth, my daughter began to wear knee pads whenever she took him for a walk. A month later, it was obvious that in order to take Lad "for a walk" a person had to be either very strong or very fast. Other evidence suggested that Lad had not been created with our family in mind. When he jumped over the backyard fence to chase a city squirrel, my suspicion was confirmed—Lad would have to go. Though the children were disappointed, they seemed to understand that Lad was a fish out of water. I placed an ad in the newspaper, and we prayed for a more suitable owner.

The first person to respond to the ad owned a home in the country with a few acres of land. He was an avid hunter. This was our man. When the prospective buyer came to look Lad over, I was dismayed when the dog jumped up to his chest and began to lick his face—one of Lad's bad habits. It wasn't the impression I had been hoping for. I was surprised when the man said, "This dog is a born hunter. I'll take him."

The point of the story is this: As we consider what our aim in life ought to be, we should consider what we were created for in the first place. Golden Labradors weren't created for city living— at least not at my house; they were made for hunting. And human beings were created for a specific purpose, too. If that purpose is ignored, we will ultimately be frustrated and miserable. The one purpose for which we were created is to love our creator.

As we observe those around us pursuing happiness, success, wealth, position, pleasure, and objectives other than loving God, it is difficult to imagine that human beings were created to love the Lord. We might concede that certain individuals with a "spiritual bend" were created to love God, but would we conclude that the whole reason for man's existence is to love his creator?

If we look to the creation account in the early chapters of Genesis, God's original intent for us becomes clearer. We see a man, Adam, who knew that God had created him. In fact, Adam walked with God and communicated directly with his creator. Adam's instincts, his intellect, emotions, and experience all confirmed the unquestioned reality: God is at the center of all things; loving him is what life is all about.

But after Adam's disobedience separated him from God, his perception became clouded. It was no less true that he was created to love God, but it was much less obvious. When we become Christians and are brought back into a relationship with God through Jesus, it is as if our sight is restored. We begin to see what has always been true; that loving God is what we were made for.

In his letter to the Ephesians, Paul writes about God's original intention for man and the fulfillment of this intention in Christ: "For he chose us in him before the creation of the world to be holy and blameless in his sight. In love he predestined us to be adopted as his sons through Jesus Christ" (Eph 1:4-5). It is a mistake to think that God's purpose for us is fulfilled when we are saved from the judgment we deserve. In fact, we are saved *in order* to be in a relationship with God, to love him as a son loves his father. It is only in loving God that we fulfill the purpose for which we were created.

We Are Commanded to Love Him

The fact that God is worthy of our love, that he loved us first and that we were created to love him, is reason enough to make loving God our ideal of life. But there is another fact to consider. The Lord does not merely inspire or encourage us to love him; he also commands us to love him.

Jesus said, "You shall love the Lord your God with all your heart, with all your soul, with all your mind and with all your strength; this is the great and the first *commandment*" (Mt 22:37-38). Later, we will consider what it means to love God with all our heart, mind, and strength. For now, I simply want to note that Jesus stated this as a command. Jesus doesn't suggest that we love God; he insists that we love him.

Commands to love are found throughout the Bible. Even so, it might seem odd for God to command us to love him if we think that love is simply a feeling—either some kind of "religious high" or a nice, warm, or affectionate feeling for God. Experience tells us that our feelings will vary. They come and go, influenced by innumerable factors, many of which appear to be outside our control. God's command to love him is not a command to feel good about him or to sustain a pious emotional state. It is a command to put him first in our lives, to be loyal and faithful, to be committed to him. Fundamentally, loving God is something we do more than something we feel. If we love God, our feelings toward him will generally be positive, but not always. If we rely on good feelings in order to love God, we will run into trouble. I will return to this point later since it has important implications. For now, it is enough to realize that loving him is something that God commands us to do.

Summary

If loving God is to be our one ideal of life, we ought to know what it is we are choosing and why. First, God is the one who is most worthy of our love. His very nature and love for us calls us to love him above all else. Second, we were created to love God; that is what we were originally designed for and the purpose for which we are reconciled to God. Third, we are commanded to love God; we shouldn't think of loving God as one of several acceptable options.

What other ideal would we want to pursue? And yet, we all know that there are some things that hold us back from wholeheartedly making this our aim. We will consider the obstacles next.

TWO

Why Not?

If loving God is your ideal, you ought to be unabashed about it. "My aim in life is to love the one who made me and saved me. I'm not saying that I can do it on my own steam, but, nonetheless, that's my ideal." Too many Christians hesitate at this point. "I know that I am supposed to love God, and deep down that's what I really want to do, but . . . ." If you've found yourself thinking something like this, you may be suffering from one or both of two attitudes. The first is called "The 'Wrong Type' Attitude," the second, "False Humility."

The Wrong Type

I hate the "wrong type" attitude! For years it kept me from confidently making loving God my aim. When I became a Christian, some of those I respected most were former drug addicts or people who were in some serious trouble before they committed their lives to the Lord. I had gotten the impression that in order to "really love God," you had to have been in bad shape before you became a Christian. As I compared my past problems with the problems of others, it started to look as though I had been a pretty mild sinner. Before long, I developed a "wrong type" attitude: Because my conversion wasn't so dramatic, I was the wrong type to love God. Worse yet, I thought I had scriptural justification for my perspective: "He who is forgiven little, loves little" (Lk 7:47). Because my past didn't seem that bad to me, I considered myself a member of the "forgiven little, loves little" club. Fortunately, something happened to open my eyes.

I went with a friend, a Christian from India, to a convention in Brooklyn, where his church had a mission center. Most of the people at the convention were older than I and most were Indians or Pakistanis. During the convention, I was asked to describe how I had become a Christian. As I told of my past life, a number of people in the audience seemed unusually impressed by what a sinner I had been. They looked very relieved when I told them of my conversion and changed life.

At first I couldn't understand their reaction. Did they respond to everyone's story this way? Was I exaggerating the negative in order to impress them? Certainly the things I mentioned about my past were wrong, but they were just the normal sins for a person my age.

Suddenly it clicked. These people were viewing my life from a different perspective. What seemed like little sins to me were big sins to them. I realized that my judgment of sin had been softened by my cultural background, in which some serious wrongdoing was regarded lightly. But my cultural bias wouldn't make much difference to a God who sees everything in untarnished objectivity. As I understood how hideous sin is in God's eyes, the passage from Luke came to mind. I hadn't been forgiven little; I had been forgiven much. I hadn't simply decided to accept the teachings of Jesus when I became a Christian. I had avoided the just wrath of God. I was qualified to love much, in spite of my earlier opinion that I was the wrong type.

There were other reasons why I didn't consider myself the type to love God. Certain aspects of my personality seemed to disqualify me. For one thing, I was (and still am) more low-key than intense. In fact, a friend once gave me a picture he had cut from the newspaper because it reminded him of me. It showed a ship traveling down a river, with the caption, "Go with the flow." Early in my Christian life, I got the impression that you had to be intense to love God. An old friend from high school, Mark, exemplified this quality. Whatever he did, he did intensely; he listened to music, read, participated in athletics, and argued *intensely*. When he gave his life to the Lord, Mark did it intensely. And from my perspective his Christian life took off. When I compared his love for God to my own, it seemed to me that he was much farther along. I attributed his growth to his intensity and concluded that you had to be intense to love God. It wasn't until I met other Christians who weren't intense, yet who obviously loved

God, that my theory fell apart. I realized that intensity had advantages and disadvantages just as being low-key did. I didn't have to become intense in order to love God.

I also thought that you had to be emotionally expressive in order to love God. Some people I knew were easily moved to tears when listening to a Christian song or hearing about God's love. Not me. Again, "not the type" was my conclusion. In fact, some of my early efforts to love the Lord were aimed at becoming more emotionally expressive. These efforts didn't meet with much success. While learning to be more expressive in praising God did help me to express my love for him, being *emotionally* expressive was neither here nor there. I was the type to love God whether or not I was emotionally expressive.

The list of wrong type attitudes is practically endless; no doubt you have your own contributions. Some people grow up with the idea that only clergymen love God; if you're not a clergyman, you're not the type to love God. Others think that in order to really appreciate God, you must be well-read and a lover of the fine arts. Or they may think that you should be sentimental and a bit introverted. But all this is sheer nonsense! Why should we put up with it? Loving God is not some mysterious ability that comes from factors like these. One type of person is able to love God: the man or woman who has been brought into a relationship with God through his only son, Jesus. If that includes you, then you are the type to love God.

False Humility

Because it often cloaks itself in Christian garb, false humility is an especially troublesome obstacle. It goes something like this: "I know that loving God is the highest aim in life, but who am I to aspire to love God?" Ironically, some people consider this attitude, which is nothing more than a low opinion of oneself, to be the Christian virtue of humility. But having a low opinion of oneself is not a virtue; it is a misunderstanding. It can keep you from embracing the ideal of life for which you were created. False humility says, "Who am I to love God?" That is an obstacle to loving God. True humility says, "I am a servant—God's servant and the servant of others." This is the path to loving God.

False humility is often expressed differently, depending on a person's Christian background. For example, many Roman Catholic friends have told me that through reading or hearing about the lives of the saints they grew up with a keen awareness of what it means to love God. Men and women like Francis of Assisi, St. Augustine, St. Clare, and St. Theresa were such spiritual giants that it seemed arrogant to aspire to their love for God. Loving God became an ideal that "humble" Christians didn't presume to take on.

False humility expressed itself differently in my own evangelical Protestant background. Having heard so much about the fact that we are sinners saved by grace (true enough) and that "in this is love, not that we loved God, but that he loved us,"

I thought that it would be prideful to say, "My aim in life is to love the Lord with all my heart, mind, and strength."

The truth is that it's never arrogant, prideful, or presumptuous to make this claim. What would Francis of Assisi say if you were to tell him, "Brother Francis, your love for God has been such an inspiration to me! In fact, so great is your love for God that I realize how presumptuous it would be of me—humble ordinary Christian that I am—to aspire to such heights. Loving God should be left to men and women of your stature." How quickly Francis would devastate such an argument.

Or imagine standing before the Lord on judgment day and saying, "I know that I am a sinner saved by grace, and that it was you who loved me first, so I did not even presume to make it my aim to love you with all my heart, mind, and strength." God preserve us from the logic of false humility!

Summary

Though we may appreciate the importance of making love for God our ideal of life, there are a variety of attitudes that make us hesitant to say, "Loving God is my aim." The "wrong type" attitude points to some personality trait or set of circumstances and says, "I am not the type to love God." False humility tricks us into thinking that it is presumptuous to make the love of God our ideal. In order to embrace the Christian ideal of life—loving God with our whole heart, mind, and strength—we have to shake off these attitudes. Every Christian can say without hesitation, embarrassment, or reserve, "Loving God is my aim."

THREE

With All Your Heart

Loving God may sound like a vague and ethereal ideal—the kind of thing that religious poets extol, but not something that you and I can hope to grasp, let alone apply to our daily lives. Indeed, loving God is deeply profound, but it is also straightforward and understandable; it has practical application for everyday life. We can understand what it means to love God and how to express this love in our lives. In fact, loving God is uncomplicated enough that we should be able to know whether or not we are doing it. The next three chapters will discuss what it means to love God with all our heart, mind, and strength. We will consider how this is expressed in some specific, practical ways.

The Heart

What does it mean to love the Lord with all of your heart? The answer of course, depends on what the heart is. Most people would describe the heart as the thing we feel with. To do something with heart is to do it "with feeling." It means that you have an emotional investment. This understanding of the heart is based on the idea that feelings represent the center of a man, the core of his being. The scripture understands the heart differently.

In the Bible, the heart is a symbol for the core of a man: The heart of a man reflects the man. But when scripture speaks of the heart, it does not focus narrowly on feelings. The heart includes intelligent thought and the will along with feelings, yet it exists at a more fundamental level than all three. The heart is the place of *fundamental choice*.

This means that we can *choose* to love God. When we make loving God our ideal, we are making a fundamental choice. The choice is fundamental because every other decision, choice, and judgment that we make is based upon it. It provides the orientation that shapes our entire life.

If we confuse the popular understanding of *heart* with the biblical view, we will get sidetracked. Instead of setting our hearts on God, we will concentrate on developing positive feelings for him, thinking that the intensity of our emotions determines the depth of our love for God. That puts the cart before the horse, since the heart—the place of fundamental choice—exists at a deeper level than feelings.

Rather than viewing love from the heart in terms of emotions, we need to understand it in a way that corresponds to the biblical perspective. We need to understand it in terms of personal commitment.

Commitment

To love the Lord with our heart is to be committed to him. Our commitment to God can be supported by our feelings, but it cannot depend on them, since commitment based only on feelings usually does not survive.

This is obviously the case in marriage. Very often one partner will develop negative feelings for the other. When this happens, the couple whose marriage is based on feelings rather than commitment may well panic. The foundation of their relationship is crumbling. Marriage requires commitment to survive. Without it, the temporary setbacks caused by fluctuating emotions will threaten the relationship.

Our love for God includes the emotions but it is *based* on commitment. It is a commitment to seek the Lord first and foremost. It is a decision to put God first, to be loyal to him, to place his will and interests above our own, no matter what.

"Putting the Lord first" is a familiar phrase, but what does it mean? A friend of mine recently reminded me. Tom went on a weekend retreat for new Christians. In the course of the weekend, he frequently expressed how good the experience was. Because I have seen people express enthusiasm before without following through, I adopted a wait-and-see attitude about the effect of the retreat on Tom's relationship with God. A week later he told me that he was no longer attending martial arts training classes. He had been very involved in the classes and enjoyed them immensely, so I was surprised at his decision. When I asked why, he told me that this particular martial arts method was very time-consuming, and it taught various "assasination skills," like ways to detach a person's liver without leaving a scratch. During the retreat he became convinced that God didn't want him to be involved in the course any longer. In giving it up, Tom was acting on his commitment to the Lord; he was loving God with his heart.

As this example illustrates, a commitment to love God involves obeying him. Jesus frequently defined love in terms of obedience. "If you love me," he told them, "you will keep my commandments" (Jn 14:15). Love simply cannot be divorced from obedience.

Our commitment to love God, to put him first, provides the foundation for our obedience. When I was a new Christian, someone told me that important decisions would be greatly simplified by making one fundamental decision: to love God above everything and to do with my life whatever the Lord wants. He was right. After I made this decision, the others that I have faced—what career to pursue, where to live, how to invest my time, how to raise my children, and so on—have become less complicated. I simply need to determine what God wants, and then do it.

For example, I had been working in the field of community mental health when I was asked to become an editor for a Christian magazine. As I thought about the offer, a number of considerations came to mind. I had been trained in mental health; editing was a whole new direction. A secular career held greater opportunities for advancement than one in a Christian organization. On the other hand, I did enjoy writing, and the idea of working with other Christians appealed to me. But was it the most responsible thing to do?

Rather than waste all of my energy struggling to balance these and other factors, I simply considered the options, prayed, and thought about what God wanted. I concluded that the Lord wanted me to work for the magazine. Because I had decided years before to put the Lord first and to obey him, it wasn't difficult to decide what to do next. The matter had already been settled in principle.

While it is always *easier* to obey God once we've decided to put his interests first, it is not always *easy* to obey. The night before his death, Jesus went to the garden of Gethsemane to pray. From the gospel narratives, it is clear that he underwent a personal struggle that night. It wasn't easy for Jesus to accept what the Father was calling him to face the next day. He obeyed, in spite of the fact that it was difficult. And the fact that it was difficult certainly didn't mean that he loved the Father any less. If anything, Jesus' love for the Father stands out all the more.

It's important to note that there are different kinds of obedience: the obedience a slave renders to his master out of fear of punishment; the obedience of an employee to an employer, motivated by the prospect of advancement; and the obedience of a son who obeys out of love for his father. It is certainly not wrong to obey God in order to avoid punishment or to receive a reward (a good son will obey for these reasons, too). However, the kind of obedience that most pleases God is the willing obedience that expresses a son's love for his father. This obedience best expresses love from the heart, love based on commitment.

Personal Commitment

While some people think of loving God primarily as an emotional experience, others view it as a rigid obligation of obedience, to be lived out with joyless severity. They see loving God as an abstraction, an impersonal command of duty. Neither view is accurate. The first group needs to learn that commitment is the basis of love for God. The second group understands the role of commitment, but they must realize that it is a *personal* commitment, one involving the whole person in a total bond.

Our love for God requires more than just adherence to a set of guidelines, laws, or principles. It isn't cold, distant, or abstract. It is a profound and total commitment to someone—not something.

Scripture emphasizes the personal nature of our love for God by describing it in terms of human relationships: father and son, husband and wife, brothers, and friends. We are sons of God, the children of our heavenly Father; we are the bride of Christ; we are related to Jesus, our elder brother; and we are called friends of God, like Abraham was. These descriptions correspond to God's original intention for us, reflected in the account of human life before the fall, when Adam and Eve "walked with God," enjoying a deep and profoundly personal communion with their Creator.

Our love for God is based on God's personal knowledge of us and on his revelation of himself to us. That's what makes this love personal. God knows us, and we can know him. This truth becomes evident when we consider the simple fact that God calls us by name and reveals his own name to us. The use of names is one of the hallmarks of a personal relationship. I see hundreds of people each week, but I don't know all of them by name. It isn't until we learn one another's names that we actually have the beginning of a personal relationship. If I forget a name, it usually means that my relationship with that person isn't very close.

In the Bible, names have even more significance. To know someone's name was to know his nature. When the Lord revealed himself to Moses as "Yahweh" or "I am who I am," he revealed his nature as well, and he brought Moses into a closer relationship with himself. It would be difficult to have a personal relationship with a nameless God or with a God we knew nothing about. The fact that he calls us by name and tells us that he knew us from the time of our conception indicates that our relationship with the almighty God is to be a personal one.

When I was considering the claims of Christianity, I was impressed by the relationship between Jesus and his early band of disciples. They were committed not merely to his ideals, teaching, or way of life. The disciples were loyal to Jesus himself. When his teaching puzzled or offended them, their personal loyalty was not shaken. Because they loved him, they stayed with him. Those who were followers of Christ because they thought he could advance their favorite cause—such as the political restoration of the kingdom to the Jewish people—eventually left. Only those who had come to know and love Jesus, who were personally committed to him remained.

Though I wanted to be this kind of disciple, I didn't understand how I could know the Lord personally. My love for God seemed more like a metaphor than a reality. My greatest desire was to have been one of the disciples who knew Jesus during his earthly ministry. "I'd give anything," I commented more than a few times, "just to meet the Lord in person, if only to shake his hand." I was thinking that in order to have a personal love for the Lord, I would have to relate to him in the natural realm, just as the apostles did before his death and resurrection.

Then I read something that Jesus told his disciples to prepare them for his death: "It is to your advantage that I go away, for if I do not go away, the Counselor will not come to you; but if I go, I will send him to you" (Jn 16:7). At first I couldn't believe what Jesus was saying. My greatest desire was to have been with Jesus as the early disciples were. Yet here was Jesus telling them that it was to their advantage for him to leave. I thought that the Lord was simply trying to help them make the best of a bad situation; but then I realized that Jesus never spoke words of idle comfort. If it had not been to their advantage for him to go, Jesus would have told them so, without sugarcoating the hard truth. No, Jesus knew that after he sent the Counselor, the Holy Spirit, his disciples would have an even deeper relationship with him. Though he would be gone, his own Spirit would be sent to live within them.

I had been longing for a personal relationship with the Lord in the natural realm, while Jesus was offering a personal relationship in the spiritual realm. This meant facing an obvious fact. Because Jesus is seated at the right hand of God in heaven, it is impossible to know him now in the natural realm; we cannot shake hands with him or talk with him as we do with each other. Instead, the Lord offers a better alternative—knowing him through the Holy Spirit, sent to us from heaven. Through the Holy Spirit, Jesus is not just close by; rather, the power of his own life is *within* us.

In order to love God on a personal level, we must enter the spiritual dimension; we must know him through the power of his Holy Spirit. It doesn't help to imagine or pretend that he is with us like other people are; nor does it square with reality. But through the Holy Spirit, Jesus makes himself known to us.

Worship and Praise: Expressing Love for God

"I appeal to you therefore, brethren, by the mercies of God, to present your bodies as a

living sacrifice, holy and acceptable to God,
which is your spiritual worship" (Rom 12:1).

According to St. Paul, worship means giving
ourselves to God. When we love the Lord with all
our heart—through our commitment to him,
through putting him first—we are worshipping
him. But worship also refers to those occasions
when we stand before the Lord to offer him a
sacrifice of praise in prayer. This kind of worship
aptly expresses the personal dimension of our love
for God, made possible through the Holy Spirit.

In my early years as a Christian, I rarely took
time to praise God in prayer. I was quick to point
out that "talk is cheap," decrying those who honor
the Lord with their lips but dishonor him with
their behavior. It was a legitimate concern. But I
was so determined not to be hypocritical that I
neglected to praise God with my lips.

One day I was reading through the book of
psalms. The psalmists impressed me by the way
they so consistently expressed their love for God
through praising him:

Praise the Lord, O my soul.
I will praise the Lord all my life;
I will sing praise to my God as long as I live.
(Ps 146:1-2)

Praise the Lord.
How good it is to sing praises to our God,
how pleasant and fitting to praise him!
(Ps 147:1)

I realized that I, too, should be able to praise God in this way, but verbalizing it was like pulling teeth. I needed help.

I sought the advice of some friends accustomed to a more openly expressive form of prayer. They spoke aloud during their private prayer and praised God by reading psalms, saying spontaneous prayers of praise, praying in tongues, or singing songs. In addition to Bible reading and prayers of petition, this kind of prayer formed an important part of their daily prayer. When I told them about my frustration in praising God, they urged me to ask the Lord to release the power of his Spirit so that I could praise and worship him more. When I did, I discovered that the Holy Spirit does provide us with the ability to praise God; as I relied more on the Spirit, it was easier to praise God.

Something else helped me: I realized that it was more important to express praise than feel it. Sometimes we think that unless we feel something, we are being insincere if we express it. But often that's not the case. Because I love my wife, it is accurate and honest for me to express my love for her, even when I may not feel especially affectionate or loving towards her. Expressing this fact does more than communicate the truth; it also strengthens our relationship. The same is true of expressing our love for God through praise. We don't have to feel love for God in order to know that we love him. As long as we are, in fact, loving God, our praise and worship is authentic.

This understanding has helped me praise God

more consistently. For instance, this morning I felt like praising God, because a friend of mine had decided that he wanted to learn more about Christianity, about what it means to make a personal commitment to the Lord. The time I had planned for prayer seemed to pass quickly. But yesterday was a different story. It was the Monday after a week's vacation—a week that went too fast. I had gone to bed late the night before and was still tired when I began to pray. I felt more like sleeping— back at our vacation spot—than praying. Nevertheless, I praised the Lord by reading some psalms, praying prayers of praise and thanksgiving, and singing. I didn't feel inspired, but I believe that this prayer was authentic, just as acceptable to God as this morning's prayer. And as a side benefit, praising God reminded me of his goodness and helped me gain the Lord's perspective on what could otherwise have been a gloomy Monday.

Summary

Our ideal of life is found in Jesus' command to "Love the Lord your God with all your heart, and with all your soul, and with all your mind" (Mt. 22:37-38). Life's highest calling, it is not an unattainable, impractical goal. First, we must understand what this ideal means. We should understand that scripture views the heart as the place of fundamental choice. We need to leave behind romantic notions that simply equate the heart with the emotions. Love from the heart can best be described as a personal commitment, similar to the love that exists between a husband and wife, or a parent and child. Our love for God involves a commitment to put him first, to seek his interests above our own. It involves obedience. It is a personal commitment like the disciples' personal love for Jesus, but mediated through the Holy Spirit. Lastly, loving God with our heart is expressed through worship and praise.

FOUR

With All Your Mind

Most of us don't view our minds as instruments with which to love God. My education—thirteen years in public schools and five at a secular university—shaped my view of the mind significantly. During this time, I learned how to think, but not once did I encounter the idea that the mind is primarily something with which we are to love and serve God.

As it turned out, I was missing the most important piece of the puzzle. When God created us in his image, he enabled us to think; he intended that our minds would love and serve him. From the Lord's perspective, a good mind is not necessarily an extremely intelligent one. Intelligence is a gift from God like any other natural gift; but God's goal is not that we have brilliant minds but that our minds become instruments for loving him. Our most important concern is not, "How can I best develop my mind?" but "How can my mind fulfill its main purpose—to love God?"

Our Minds: Subject to God

As a young teenager I read some books by Ayn Rand. Her writings convinced me that Christianity wasn't true—a conclusion I reached with my mind. Years later, I finally read one of the gospels. I realized that Christianity made more sense than I had given it credit for. In the first instance, my mind had been engaged in the process that led to spiritual death, and in the second, in the process that led to life. Even now I find that I can apply my brainpower to help solve a tough problem one moment and then to think up some clever rationalization for wrongdoing the next.

On a larger scale, men and women have applied their minds to extremely difficult problems and come up with extraordinary answers. From the discovery of radium to the increasingly refined techniques of neurosurgery, evidence shows that our minds are equipped to deal with tremendously complex situations. But for every wonder performed, the human mind has contributed a horror: Hitler's Third Reich, nuclear bombs, biological warfare. Our minds are powerful tools, tools that can either serve God or work against him. Regardless of how dazzling the power of the brain is, once we stray from the plan of God, our minds can become instruments of destruction, a curse rather than a blessing. In order to love God with these minds of ours, we must submit them to God.

The question we ought to ask is not, "What seems best to me?," but, "What does God think of this?" If we approach life this way, our ideas about what is right and wrong will change. For example, I used to think that it was okay to speak against others; if I had a negative opinion about them, I wasn't reluctant to offer it. I realized that this could easily get out of hand, so I tried not to be malicious, but in many cases it seemed innocent and harmless enough. Then I came across the word "slander" in the Bible. It was located in some very disturbing contexts (such as a list of sins that can keep one out of the kingdom of God). As I studied the biblical view of slander, I realized that my standards were wrong. Things that I thought were "innocent and harmless enough" the Lord considered serious sin. I changed my mind about the matter.

Admittedly, we can't always know what God thinks about a particular issue, just as we don't always know what Jesus would do in a given situation. For example, though I now have a much clearer understanding of what constitutes slander, there are still some complicated questions to which the answers are not obvious. But by and large we *can* discover God's perspective on how we ought to live. We know that God is against murder, stealing, adultery, and some other things. We know that he wants us to be loyal to him and to other Christians; he wants children to obey parents and to care for them as they grow older, and so on. While many people are confused about these questions, we need not succumb to ethical paralysis. At the very least, when we face the stickier issues, the answer to the question, "What does God think about this?" ought to be the one to most satisfy our minds.

The Deciding Opinion

Considering what God thinks about a given issue means more than simply consulting him. Often when we ask for advice, we are merely requesting someone's opinion. We respect them, so we want to consider their point of view. If we have doubts about their advice, we get a second opinion. For example, my daughter was having chronic ear infections. The pediatrician suggested that we consult an otorhinolaryngologist. After consulting a medical dictionary to find out that an otorhinolaryngologist was an ear, nose, and throat specialist, we took her to this doctor for a consultation. He recommended surgery. But before I agreed to this, I asked to see a doctor specializing in allergies, a possible cause of the infections. This approach was fine with the ear, nose, and throat specialist. He knew that he was just a consultant, and he welcomed second opinions.

God, however, does not consider himself a consultant. He does not give opinions or "input;" he gives authoritative direction, not only concerning what we should do but also what we should think. If we treat God's word merely as a valuable point of view, we are not loving him with our minds.

Before I was a Christian, I read the gospel according to Matthew and was impressed with Jesus' teaching, until I came to his views on divorce. "Too harsh," I thought, "unrealistic. What about all the people who are mismatched and miserable because of it?" That disagreement ended my interest in the Bible for the time being. I had consulted the teaching of Christ and found it not entirely to my liking; so I ignored it. I didn't accept Jesus' thoughts as authoritative direction; I didn't change the way I looked at divorce. Because I did not come to God's word with a Christian attitude, my mind was no more Christian for the encounter. A Christian is committed to change his mind whenever he discovers that one of his own opinions or viewpoints differs from Christ's thinking.

Everyday Use

"Once I'm convinced that God thinks differently than I do about a particular subject, it isn't difficult for me to change my mind. However, I usually find it much harder to keep my thoughts from straying or from mulling over things that don't help me do what he wants." This comment highlights something many of us have experienced: the challenge of keeping our thoughts "on track." Listening to a sermon on Sunday morning, we find our minds concentrating on last night's crossword puzzle or thinking ahead to a meeting at work on Monday. Though we've decided to love someone whom we consider it difficult to love, we find our thought dwelling on their shortcomings whenever we are with that person. The Lord assures us that he has forgiven us for a recent sin, yet our minds won't let it drop. Often it seems that our minds frustrate rather than foster our love for God. What can we do about it?

You've probably noticed that some ways of thinking don't change instantly, even though you've decided to submit them to the Lord. Our minds have been formed over a period of time to work the way they do. Circumstances, families, friends, the media—all are part of a process that trains our minds. Some patterns of thought are like bad habits; they frustrate God's work in us and they are often hard to break.

We are able to break some bad habits with relative ease, even when they are firmly entrenched. More often though, we have to undergo a process of unlearning and retraining. When I first learned to play paddleball, I never developed a backhand shot. Instead, I simply switched the paddle to my left hand whenever the ball came to my left side. After I mastered this technique, another player told me that it was illegal: The paddle had to stay in the same hand throughout the game. This was a real blow to my game. Not only did I have to learn how to make a backhand shot; I had to teach myself not to switch hands. For a while I was a pushover on the left side. When the ball came in that direction, my left hand would automatically grab the paddle while my right resisted this illegal act.

Working on the Railroad

The following analogy may help us understand how our minds can develop bad habits and how the retraining process can change them. We can think of our minds as a railroad system, with railroad tracks connecting innumerable points. Each track represents a series of thoughts that tend to become associated with each other. A particular route or line represents a length of track connecting two points: a point of departure and a destination. Some of these routes have been laid down beforehand by the World, Flesh, and the Devil Railways, Inc. Take, for example, the line that we might call "negativity."

Our "train of thought" might depart from the station called, "God does not love me." Its destination is "Give Up!" The track consists of a sequence of thoughts that have become habitual over the years, thanks to the careful maintenance of WF&D Railways.

When we suspect that our thoughts are headed in an undesirable direction, we ought to ask ourselves a couple of questions: (1) Where did this line of thinking originate?, and (2) Where is this line of thinking headed—what is its ultimate destination? Sometimes the individual thoughts that constitute a particular track seem innocent enough; the answers to these two questions will help us see the route's true colors.

For example, imagine that you are beginning to think that a number of people close to you don't really care about you. The more you think about it, the longer the list grows. When you pause for a moment, you realize that the end of that line of thinking is further separation from others. Is that where you want to go? Is that where the Lord is leading you? And where did that line of thinking originate? You may realize that the point of departure was something like hurt feelings because a friend ignored you in some small way. If the latter

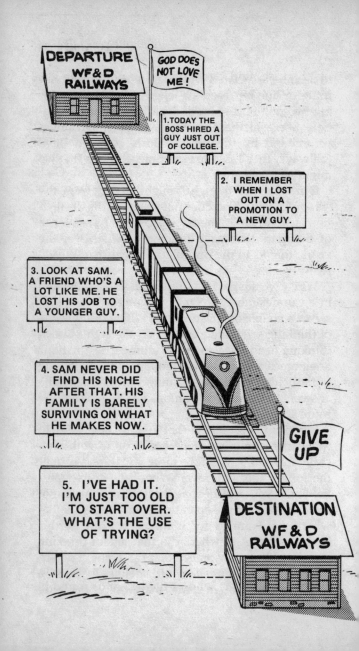

is the case, find God's departure point—the ideal of serving others which replaces self-concern—then abandon the other route entirely in order to think along a different line.

The key to breaking bad patterns of thought is not to be found in any particular technique, per se. More important is the realization that with God's help we can influence what goes on in our minds.

One woman I know was troubled by the way her mind worked at times. Faced with a relatively minor problem, she would dwell on its most negative aspects, imagining the worst possible outcome until it loomed in her mind as a major difficulty. When I pointed this out, she replied, "That's the way my mind has always worked. There's nothing I can do about it!" The idea that she could significantly influence the direction of her thoughts was totally new to her.

Though her early efforts to change her thoughts met with only modest success, it was enough to convince her that what transpired in her mind was not completely outside her control. Now, when faced with the same tendency to dwell on the negative, she steps back and says to herself, "Aha! Here I go again, exaggerating how bad things are and imagining the worst possible outcome. Lord, I know it can't be as bad as I think; help me to gain your perspective."

Mind Care

Recently I read about Ern Baxter, a respected Christian teacher, who at the age of 65 found his health deteriorating rapidly. His blood pressure was high, along with his blood sugar, and he was having signs of an impending heart attack. The prospect of ending his active ministry because of poor physical condition motivated him to take some steps to improve his health. He eliminated cafeine from his diet, lost several pounds, and changed some poor eating habits. Under a doctor's supervision he began a regular exercise program; he also got to bed earlier and slept a full seven hours per night, which was more than he had been accustomed to.

After a while on this regimen, his health improved considerably. His blood pressure came down, and he no longer needed insulin to control his blood sugar level. Having regained much of his former physical strength and vitality, he was able to continue his active Christian service.

Reverend Baxter's experience illustrates the importance of taking care of ourselves so that our bodies can serve our aim of loving God. The same is true for our minds; if our minds are to support our life's aim, we will have to care for them properly. In so doing, we can avoid problems with our thoughts, such as those discussed in earlier examples.

Like the rest of our body, our mind is greatly affected by what goes into it. Of course, we don't have complete control over what goes into our minds, and our minds are not so tender that we have to create a "spiritual hothouse" in which every environmental factor is closely monitored. But we do have some degree of influence over a number of significant factors.

One area we cannot afford to neglect concerns our use of the media—television, radio, reading material, and so on. If our minds are bombarded by the false view of reality so often portrayed in the media, we shouldn't be surprised when, as a result, temptation, doubt, anxiety, and self-concern flourish in us. We ought to exercise careful judgment about our use of the media. Why should we let our minds be taken up with a view of reality and a set of values that we know is riddled with falsehood? In recent years, I've cut my time in front of the television drastically; and I'm much choosier about what I will watch, listen to on the radio, and read. Since I've begun to exercise more control over the media's influence, my mind is much less prone to distraction, passivity, and other effects produced or encouraged by excessive exposure to the media.

Discipline is another aspect of caring for our minds. Among other things, it means learning to say "no." In *The Wisdom of the Desert*, a collection of sayings and stories from a group of early Christians who lived a life of prayer and solitude in the desert, a young monk approaches an older one and asks for advice about how to handle the many distracting thoughts that fill his mind. The elder instructs him to go outside, hold open his garment around his chest, and catch the wind. When the younger hermit reports that this is impossible, the elder tells him that it is also impossible to keep all distracting thoughts from entering his mind. But, he adds, "Your job is to say no to them."

Loving God's Word

So far, we've considered our minds from two perspectives: (1) Where we stand on important issues (our perspective and opinions), and (2) How our minds work from moment to moment. In each case, God's word in scripture is the key to loving God with our minds.

Why, we might ask, is the Bible so important in our ability to love God with our minds? The answer is found in the Christian belief that the Bible contains the word of God. Paul wrote to the Christians in Thessalonika, "And we also thank God constantly for this, that when you received the word of God which you heard from us, you accepted it not as the word of men but as what it really is, the word of God, which is at work in you believers" (1 Thes 2:13). Paul was grateful that the Thessalonians hadn't received the gospel simply as the word of men, but as the word of God. They realized that Paul's message should not be ignored or disobeyed because it was, in fact, God's word; it was an expression of God himself.

The Jews of ancient Israel were known as, "The people of the Book." They belived that to honor, love, and obey the sacred scripture was to honor, love, and obey God himself. To neglect, defile, or despise the scripture was to do the same to God. This same regard for scripture ought to character-ize the people of the new covenant.

It is possible, of course, to read the Bible like we read any other book—as literature or religious history and nothing more. But if we don't read the

Bible as God's word to us, we might as well not read it. I knew an English professor who, because he loved the prose of the King James Version, read the Bible more than many Christians. But because he didn't love God, he missed the whole point. He didn't read the scripture as God's word.

We will obey the teaching of the Bible if we read it as God's word. We won't think of it simply as one among many voices but will seek and follow its instruction. We will expect God to reveal himself and will find that he gives us strength, wisdom, and direction through his word.

Practically Speaking

In order to love God's word with our minds, we can do a number of specific things.

Regular Reading

I know a man who decided to spend at least fifteen minutes each day reading the Bible. He's been doing that for fifteen years now and claims that it's one of the best decisions he ever made.

Our desire to read scripture plays an important role, but we must also develop the habit of reading the Bible. My appetite for food is incorporated into the habit of eating three meals a day. This provides a good pattern for my eating. Of course, there's nothing sacred about it; other cultures have developed other eating habits which work equally well. The point is this: By developing a regular pattern, human beings are able to insure that important things are not neglected or crowded out by other demands.

During my regular prayer time each morning, I have developed the habit of reading scripture. Some people take other times—such as the lunch hour, or just before turning in at night. Regardless of which pattern works best, we should all try to develop some habits for reading scripture regularly. Otherwise, more pressing or attractive (but less important) demands are likely to distract us.

If you haven't read much scripture, there is another lesson to be drawn from the way our natural appetite for food works. My children don't have much of a taste for vegetables; but they eat them because they must. They also tend to enjoy fewer kinds of food than I do. If they are like most people, they will acquire a taste for more foods as they grow older. Who knows? In ten years, mushrooms and kidney bean salad may be among their favorites. In a similar way, I've learned to appreciate different books in the Bible that at first were difficult for me to handle.

When I first committed my life to the Lord, I decided to read the Bible from cover to cover. My desire was good, but the strategy was bad. Reading the first few chapters of Genesis precipitated a major crisis in my immature faith. I became entangled in a web of questions I couldn't answer. Was Eve really created from Adam's rib? Were Adam and Eve real people or representative? What about evolution? I talked to an older Christian who answered some of my questions about Genesis, and then gave me even better advice: "Stick with the gospels for a few months, then read the book of Acts; when you're ready for the Old Testament, start with the Psalms, and then we'll talk about how they apply to the Christian." As my faith matured, I was able to receive God's word from an increasing number of books in the Bible. It wasn't that I had to personally canonize each book before I accepted it as God's word. Early in my Christian life, I realized that all of scripture was God's word, but it took time for my spiritual appetite for different books of the Bible to develop.

More in Depth Study When Possible

I recently read *The Chosen*, a novel about a father and son who were Orthodox Jews. On the Sabbath day, they spent an hour or two studying scripture together; sometimes they spent the whole afternoon discussing a few verses. Their example inspired me to take time for Bible study with my son and to look for more opportunities to study scripture in depth. But there was something even more inspiring about the book: the way the men in the novel viewed the study of the Torah (the books of the Law) as an expression of love for God.

Our goal is not to become great "Bible experts." We should study scripture primarily as a way to love the Lord, who is himself the Word made flesh. When we study the Bible, we ought to be motivated by a desire to understand more about God's ways so that we can conform to them, and by a desire to know God as he is revealed in his word. Scripture study can be an academic exercise like any other, but it is meant to be an avenue leading to a deepened relationship with God.

The time available for study will vary from person to person. It might be an hour each week or an evening each month. A variety of methods can be used, from studying a small section—one chapter, or just a few verses—to studying a particular theme that appears throughout the Bible. It can be very helpful to read introductory and background information. Material of this sort would include introductions to each of the books in the Bible, information about the culture and times of the Old and New Testaments, and facts about how the Bible came into existence.

Hearing the Scriptures Read and Taught About

Currently millions of copies of the Bible exist, but in the time of the early church this was not the case (just as it is not the case in many parts of the world today). Christians had to rely more on *hearing* the word of God—usually during the public reading of scripture or by means of teaching or preaching based on the scriptures. I've found that hearing scripture read aloud—especially during a worship service will often have greater impact than if I read the passage myself. This shouldn't be too surprising. After all, much of the Bible is derived from an oral tradition, designed specifically for hearing. The Bible is often addressed to a group of believers, (e.g., the letters of St. Paul), a factor which makes hearing the scriptures with other Christians especially appropriate.

Another good way to receive God's word is to listen to teaching or preaching based on the Bible. A gifted teacher or preacher can draw out the spiritual meaning of a particular passage in order to apply it to the lives of his listeners, increasing their faith in the process. "So faith comes from what is heard, and what is heard comes by the preaching of Christ" (Rom 10:17).

Praying the Prayers of Scripture

In his first letter to the Corinthians, Paul refers to "praying with the mind" (1 Cor 14:15). A good way to pray with our minds is to pray the prayers of scripture. I once went through the book of Revelation and underlined all the prayers of the heavenly host. Every now and then I'll open to Revelation and pray these inspiring prayers.

Praying biblical prayers is an excellent way to learn how to pray. For example, we might wonder how we can express the personal nature of our love for God without being sentimental. Psalm 116 provides an excellent model:

> I love the Lord, because he hears
> My voice and my supplications.
> Because he has inclined his ear to me.
> Therefore I shall call upon him as long as I
>   live. . . .
> What shall I render to the Lord
> For all his benefits toward me?
> I shall lift up the cup of salvation,
> And call upon the name of the Lord
> (Ps 116:1-2, 12-13).

Summary

God's purpose for our minds is fulfilled only when we use them as instruments for loving him. We love God with our minds by thinking as he thinks. His perspective on life ought to determine ours. In other words, to love God with our minds means that our minds are subject to God. This ideal ought to shape the way we think from moment to moment. Some patterns of thought may be like bad habits, which don't fit our ideal. With God's help, those habits can be broken. We ought to care for our minds so that they don't become full of things that keep us from loving God. In all of these matters, God's word in scripture provides the key to loving him with our minds. It's important that we take steps to bring our minds into contact with God's word. Because his word is an expression of God himself, we ought to love, respect, and obey it.

FIVE

With All Your Strength

Jesse Owens, the winner of four gold medals in the 1936 Olympic Games, learned an important lesson in one of his first high school races. He was near the finish line, with a few other runners in close pursuit, when he did something that a good runner never should. Owens grit his teeth, and set a tense, fierce, determined look on his face. He tried to win the race with a show of outward determination and strength. He lost.

Before the next meet, Owens' coach took him to a horse race. The young athelete noticed that the fastest horses didn't appear to be straining at all. They didn't waste their energy on fierce, determined facial expressions. Yet, even though they look relaxed, they were giving everything they had to the race.

It is easy to confuse loving God with all our strength with the same kind of teeth-gritting intensity that Jesse tried to use. However, that kind of intensity won't help. Only one thing is required if we are to love the Lord with all our strength: everything. Love for God requires that we give all our resources—time, money, energy, possessions, gifts, and abilities—to him.

No Limits on Love

The Lord does not ask us to give him "everything, except . . ." or "all, but . . . ." Just as his "yes" means "yes," his "all" means "all." If we set any limits whatsoever, no matter how reasonable or generous they may seem, we are simply not loving God with all our strength.

This sounds like an extraordinary requirement. Actually it is the kind of requirement we ought to expect. Even human relationships call for much, if not all of our resources. A husband's commitment to his wife means that his resources belong to her. If he has to work two full-time jobs in order to provide food for the family, he does it. If he inherits a fortune, the money belongs to his wife as well. We don't think of this as an extraordinary level of commitment for a Christian marriage; it is just what we would expect. When the Lord says, "Everything that you have belongs to me," he is making a statement about the kind of relationship that exists between us. It is a relationship of total commitment, a relationship in which nothing is withheld.

If there is ever any question about whether or not something we possess ought to be available to the Lord, the answer is always yes.

The Spiritual Vitality Test

One of the most accurate ways to measure spiritual vitality in a Christian group is to look at how the members spend their time and money. If most of their extra time and money is spent on themselves, something isn't working right. Time and money are two of our most common and valuable resources; together they constitute a sizable portion of our "strength."

Money Matters

Some Christians, reacting to past experiences in churches that overemphasized monetary needs, think that it's "unspiritual" to talk about money. It is true that God does not need our money; in that sense money doesn't matter to him. But he is interested in how we use money.

Jesus said, "Where your treasure is, there will your heart be also" (Mt 6:21). The use of our money is not a side issue. What we do with what we possess reflects the condition of our heart—who we are and what we want on the deepest level.

Good Management

The first thing a Christian has to learn about his money is that he doesn't own it; instead, he manages it. Money is simply a token of some material resource or the service of other human beings. Strictly speaking, these resources, whether gold, silver, land, or someone else's time aren't ours in anything but a legal sense. We did not make them—they were here before we came and will remain after we are gone; and we cannot take them with us. The one who created these things retains ownership over them.

God has given us everything we have, including our money. It's our responsibility to manage it well. A good manager has the interests of the owner in mind. My father-in-law, for example, works for a division of General Motors, the American automaker. His performance as a manager is based on how well he advances the interests of the company with the resources that the company has given him. He works with the department that manufactures the company's prototype cars. He can't spend company resources on projects that aren't in the company interests. If he were to manufacture a splendid prototype submarine, just because he liked submarines, he wouldn't be considered a great manager. In fact, he'd probably lose his job.

As good managers of money, we should be using it according to God's interests. For one person, God's interest might best be served by voluntary poverty, such as Francis of Assisi practiced. For another, God's interests would be best advanced if the person were earning a high income as the president of a company.

The father of ten children, who earns an income of $20,000 per year, might have to spend almost all of it on his family. A single man earning the same income might be able to give much more to the poor or to support Christian missionaries, for example. Both men could be managing their money according to God's interests, doing what the Lord wants with their income.

Tithing

When a new Christian asks me how to manage his finances in a Christian way, I usually recommend that he begin by giving one-tenth of his income to the church. This practice is called tithing. Scripture refers to the tithe as the "first fruits"; the first thing we do with the income God has given us is to return a portion of it to him. "The first fruits of the ground you shall bring to the house of the Lord your God" (Ex 34:36).

The tithe is not the 10 percent left over after all other expenses are met. It is the *first* 10 percent; and in the case of an agricultural economy, it was the *best* portion of the produce. When we give the first and best portion of our income, we acknowledge that everything we have belongs to God. Through the prophet Haggai, the Lord declared, "The silver is mine, and the gold is mine" (Hg 2:8). We are mistaken if we think that God needs our silver and gold; the tithe doesn't represent a tax for services rendered. Rather, by tithing we return to God part of what he gives us, in order to express his ownership of all that we have. We see this in Malachi's prophecy:

"Return to me, and I will return to you, says the Lord of hosts. But you say, 'How shall we return?' Will man rob God? Yet you are robbing me. But you say, 'How are we robbing thee?' In your tithes and offerings. You are cursed with a curse, for you are robbing me; the whole nation of you. Bring the full tithes into the storehouse, that there may be food in my house, and thereby put me to the test, says the Lord of hosts, if I will not open the windows of heaven for you and pour down for you an overflowing blessing (Mal 3:7-10)."

The Lord considered the tithe to be money given directly to him. In the Old Testament, the tithes were brought to the temple; they were the basic provision for its maintenance. The tithe did not include other forms of giving, such as almsgiving; it was money given "to the Lord" by way of the temple. Under the new covenant, the temple is the body of believers where God is present in a special way. Giving 10 percent of our income to the church does not constitute philanthropy; we are simply fulfilling our financial responsibility. Our giving ought to go beyond the tithe—to support the Lord's work beyond our church and to provide for those in need.

If you want to manage your money with God's interests in mind, if you want to express the fact that everything you have belongs to him, tithing is a good place to begin.

Generous Giving

Francis of Assisi gave all his money to the poor and then made a vow of poverty himself. John Wesley said, "Earn all you can, save all you can (that is, don't waste money), and give all you can." Francis and Wesley had two different approaches, but both approaches are good Christian approaches, depending on God's will for a particular individual. Generous giving is central to both.

Generous giving is part of good money management because it reflects the policy of the owner, who is himself generous. All who work for him ought to be generous too. St. Paul described generous giving in his second letter to the Corinthians:

"We want you to know, brethren, about the grace of God which has been shown in the churches of Macedonia, for in a severe test of affliction, their abundance of joy and their extreme poverty have overflowed in a wealth of liberality on their part. For they gave according to their means, as I can testify, and beyond their means, of their own free will begging us earnestly for the favor of taking part in the relief of the saints" (2 Cor 8:1-4).

Paul was raising money for the needy believers in Jerusalem, who were faced with famine. In his appeal to the Corinthians, he described the generous giving of the Christians in Macedonia, noting three different aspects of their liberality:

1. *They gave, according to their means.* Paul didn't say, "The Macedonians contributed $5,000—can you match that?" He said, "The Macedonians gave according to their means—you should do likewise." The Macedonians' generosity was like that of the widow in the temple who caught Jesus' attention.

> And he sat down opposite the treasury, and
> watched the multitude putting money into the
> treasury. Many rich people put in large sums.
> And a poor widow came, and put in two copper
> coins, which make a penny. And he called his
> disciples to him and said to them, "Truly I say to
> you, this poor widow has put in more than all
> those who are contributing to the treasury. For
> they all contributed out of their abundance; but
> she out of her poverty has put in everything she
> had, her whole living" (Mk 12:41-44).

The Macedonians didn't necessarily contribute a
large sum of money; but they became a model of
generosity, because their "extreme poverty" overflowed in a wealth of liberality. . . . For they gave
according to their means. . . ."

2. *They gave extravagantly*. Not only did the Macedonians give "according to their means;" they
even gave "beyond their means." The generosity
that Paul pointed to as an example was overflowing, erring, if it were possible, on the side of
liberality. Their gift was more than a measured,
reasonably generous amount in light of their
means. This kind of giving is closest to the generosity of God himself, who in giving his only Son,
gave extravagantly and unexpectedly.

3. *They gave freely*. The believers in Macedonia
weren't pressured or cajoled into contributing to
the needs of the saints in Jerusalem. They gave,
"of their own free will." It was something they did
eagerly, not begrudgingly. In fact, Paul says that
the Macedonians begged them for the opportu-

nity. This voluntary, unreluctant giving is the kind that most pleases the Lord. As Paul said, "God loves a cheerful giver" (2 Cor 9:7).

Time

Time is the universal resource. While some people simply don't have any money to manage, everyone has time. The same two principles that apply to loving God with our money also apply to loving God with our time: (1) We don't own our time; we manage it, and (2) The Lord wants us to be generous with our time.

Whose Time?

C.S. Lewis, in *The Screwtape Letters*, describes the folly of thinking that our time is our own. The book is a fictitious collection of letters from a demon named "Screwtape" to his demon-nephew, "Wormwood." Uncle Screwtape, who is schooling Wormwood in the art of tempting men away from God, writes:

> Now you will have noticed that nothing throws him [the Christian being tempted] into a passion so easily as to find a tract of time which he reckoned on having at his own disposal unexpectedly taken from him. It is the unexpected visitor (when he looked forward to a tête-à-tête with his friend) that throws him out of gear. Now he is not yet so uncharitable or slothful that these small demands on his courtesy are in

themselves too much for it. They anger him because he regards his time as his own and feels that it is being stolen. You must therefore zealously guard in his mind the curious assumption, "My time is my own." Let him have the feeling that he starts each day as the lawful possessor of twenty-four hours. Let him feel as a grievous tax that portion of his property which he has to make over to his employers, and as a generous donation that further portion which he allows to religious duties. But what he must never be permitted to doubt is that the total from which these deductions have been made was, in some mystical sense, his own personal birthright.

You have a difficult task. The assumption which you want him to go on making is so absurd that, if once questioned, even we cannot find a shred of argument in its defense. The man can neither make, nor retain, one moment of time; it all comes to him by pure gift; he might as well regard the sun and moon as his chattels.

We are managers, not owners of our time. To love the Lord with this portion of our strength is to manage our time according to the owner's interests. For some people, God's interests are best served if they spend several hours a week engaged in some kind of obvious Christian service, such as evangelism. The Lord may want others to invest more time working in a secular job or studying. I know a young man named Randy who, as a premed college student, renewed his commitment to

Christ. He was in the habit of spending most of his waking hours studying. The Lord directed him to cut down on his study time in order to devote more time to Christian fellowship and telling other students about Christianity. For the last two years of undergraduate studies and the first year of medical school he did this. On the average, he studied much less than his classmates and got better grades as well. In his second year of medical school, it became clear to Randy that the Lord wanted him to spend more time studying and less in more explicitly Christian service. The adjustment was more difficult for Randy because he was in the habit of thinking that the more time one spends in direct Christian service, the more one is loving God. In various ways the Lord reminded him, "Your love for me is not measured by how many hours you spend doing Christian things; you are doing what I want with your time and that's the important thing."

What Do You Do With Your Free Time?

Most people have some time during the week which they consider free. For the working person, this usually falls in the evening and on the weekend. This time provides us with a special opportunity for expressing our love for God. In most cases, some of it ought to be invested in a form of Christian service. If you spend all your free time on yourself, then you are probably not loving the Lord with all your strength.

Christian service can refer to a wide range of

activities: visiting the sick, helping those in need, evangelizing others, and serving the spiritual and practical needs of fellow Christians. Christian service is not necessarily "spiritual;" often it is mundane. I spent one evening a week for over a year setting up chairs for a large prayer meeting; for another two hours a week, I helped out in the mail room of a Christian magazine. No matter what opportunities for service are available, the Lord wants us to be generous with our free time.

Summary

Loving God with all our strength is the final aspect of our ideal of life. Our "strength" refers to our resources: money, time, possessions—everything we have. To love God with these things, we must first realize that all that we have comes from God. He owns it in the first place. Our job is to manage it well, with his interests in mind. And we ought to be generous with these things, not claiming them for our own, but making them available to God. If we manage our resources according to God's interests and if we are generous with whatever he has given us, whether small or great, we are loving God with our strength.

SIX

How Is It Possible?

Some men and women in Jesus' day wanted to love God with all of their heart, mind, and strength. They reminded themselves daily of their aim in life, this "yoke of the kingdom:" "Hear O Israel! The Lord our God is one. And you shall love the Lord your God with all your heart, and with all your soul, and with all your strength." But in spite of their efforts to live by this ideal, they were frustrated, blocked by an obstacle they could not remove.

The rabbis told a story describing this frustration and pointing to the answer. They spoke of a road running through a town; in the middle of the road lay a huge boulder that no one could budge. One day the king of that land came to the people and said, "Chip away at that boulder for the time being, but the day is coming when I will remove it from your midst."

"So shall it be," said the rabbis, "that at the coming of the Messiah the obstacle will be removed from your midst."

If we try to live the ideal of loving God simply by exerting our willpower and taking it upon our own shoulders, we will find ourselves no more effective than those townspeople chipping away at the boulder in the road. We will soon discover that this "yoke" is too heavy for us. It will only frustrate and eventually crush us.

Jesus provided another way when he said, "Come to me, all whose work is hard, whose load is heavy; and I will give you relief. Bend your necks to *my yoke*, and learn from me, for I am gentle and humble-hearted; and your souls will find relief. For my yoke is good to bear, my load is light" (Mt 11:28-30).

The yoke of Jesus was the yoke of the kingdom of heaven, just as he had learned it from his earthly father, "Shema Israel. . . ." But the way to pick up this yoke is found in the words, "Come to me." As we come to Jesus and enter into a relationship with him, we can carry the yoke, because the power of the Holy Spirit makes it light. This is the answer to our frustration referred to in the prophets: a new relationship with God in the power of his Holy Spirit.

"Behold, the days are coming, says the Lord, when I will make a new covenant with the house of Israel and the house of Judah, not like the covenant which I made with their fathers when I took them by the hand to bring them out of the land of Egypt, my covenant which they broke, though I was their husband, says the Lord. . . . I will put my law within them, and I will write it upon their hearts; and I will be their God, and they shall be my people. And no longer shall each man teach his neighbor and

each his brother, saying, 'Know the Lord,' for
they shall all know me, from the least of them to
the greatest, says the Lord.'"

(Jer 31:31-34)

This new relationship was to be a close, personal
relationship in which the people would know their
God; it would be based on a law written on their
hearts.

How this new relationship would be possible is
also described. "A new heart I will give you,"
prophesied Ezekiel, "and a new spirit I will put
within you. . . . I will put my spirit within you, and
cause you to walk in my statutes" (Ez 36:26-27).
And from Joel, "It shall come to pass afterward,
that I will pour out my spirit on all flesh" (Jl 2:28).

In order to love God with all our heart, mind,
and strength, we must learn to rely on the power
of the Holy Spirit, the same Spirit that Jesus gives
us when we come to him. It is like learning to ride
a bicycle; you've got to rely on something you can't
see, but which you know is there.

I remember learning to ride a bike when I was
about six years old. My father told me what to do,
explaining each step carefully. I understood his
instructions perfectly. I looked around and saw
plenty of other kids riding bicycles. But when I had
all the instructions down pat and was up on that
seat for my first test run, I had one more question:
"How can I do this?" From that vantage point,
riding a bicycle looked like an impossible task.

There is a good reason why riding a bicycle is
not impossible. It is called inertia, a law of physics

which everyone who rides a bike learns at least
intuitively to rely on. The law of inertia states that
objects in motion tend to stay in motion. Once
you've reached a certain speed on a bicycle, the
bike will tend to keep going. Part of the thrill of
riding a bike for the first time is discovering inertia
in action; once you get going it works! Just as God
has provided physical laws, like inertia, which
make bicycling possible, he has provided something which makes it possible for us to love him.
That something is neither a law, nor a principle,
but a someone: the Holy Spirit. The Holy Spirit
enables us to love God. And just as the bicyclist
must rely on inertia, which he cannot see, those
who love God must rely on another force which
cannot be seen, yet which exists nonetheless. The
Holy Spirit is an objective reality—something that
was once outside of us, but now lives within us.

Jesus once taught a Samaritan woman about the
gift of his life within us. She was drawing water
from Jacob's well, pulling it up perhaps as far as
one hundred feet by bucket, when Jesus asked her
for a drink. This is how their conversation went:

"You are a Jew and I am a Samaritan woman.
How can you ask me for a drink?"

Jesus answered her, "If you knew the gift of
God and who it is that asks you for a drink, you
would have asked him and he would have given
you living water."

"Sir," the woman said, "you have nothing to
draw with and the well is deep. Where can you
get this living water? Are you greater than our

father Jacob, who gave us the well and drank from it himself, as did also his sons and his flocks and herds?"

Jesus answered, "Everyone who drinks this water will be thirsty again, but whoever drinks the water I give him will never thirst. Indeed, the water I give him will become in him a spring of water welling up to eternal life" (Jn 4:9-14).

From the beginning of the conversation, it is clear that Jesus has more in mind for the woman than she can imagine. After asking for a drink of water from the well and hearing her reply, Jesus tells the woman that she could receive "living water" from him. This sounds like an unusual offer to us, but at the time, "living water" was the term used for running water or fresh water—the kind you would find in a well or a stream rather than from a stagnant source. The woman's response ("How can you do that without a bucket?") made sense.

But then Jesus revealed that what he had in mind was better than the water from the well. To get the water from Jacob's well, you had to pull it out bucket by bucket. The water Jesus spoke of was like a "spring of water, welling up." It was like the water from a different kind of well than Jacob's, called an artesian well. An artesian well was tapped into an underground spring, and the water did "well up" to the surface, providing a continuous and accessible flow of fresh water. You didn't need to lower a bucket one hundred feet and pull it up every time, because the well was like a continuously flowing fountain.

This spring of living water, of course, represents the Holy Spirit. It is this source, God's Spirit within us, that provides us with love for God. It is not just a source that we must labor to receive, like the woman pulling water out of Jacob's well, but a source within us that is like an overflowing fountain.

Before we received the Holy Spirit, we were like the Samaritan woman: Our capacity to love God was determined by our own human limitations. But God's gift changed all that. Though our own capacity for loving God may be small, our love for God need not be small, because God has placed within us a source that more than makes up for our lack.

CONCLUSION

It is possible to love God. It is possible for *you* to love God. The same ideal that the great Christians of history have lived for can be yours as well. If you thought that you weren't the type to love him or that loving God was too high or grandiose an aim for you, you were wrong. You were made to love God. It is the only thing worth living for, and it's what God commands you to do.

The ideal of loving God with all your heart, mind, and strength isn't nearly as vague or impractical as you might have thought. It involves specific, practical actions, decisions, and commitments. But you can't love God by simply applying your will and deciding to do it. Whoever tries to love God like that will fail. Jesus showed us the way when he said, "If anyone is thirsty, let him come to me and drink, and out of his heart shall flow rivers of living water." The power of the Holy Spirit enables us to love God.

An ideal for a select few, beyond the reach of all but a handful of spiritual giants? No. Loving God should be the ideal for every one of us. A lofty ideal beyond our grasp? Before the death and resurrection of Jesus and the outpouring of his Holy Spirit, it was, but no longer. Now you and I can love God with a love as great as his gift.

The books in the Living as a Christian Series can be used effectively in groups. To receive a free copy of the Leader's Guide to this book and the others in the series, send a stamped, self-addressed business envelope to Servant Books, Box 8617, Ann Arbor, Michigan 48107.